Map Legend

Borders

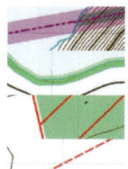

- Country border
- Natural Park border
- Military/restricted area
- Fence
- Gate

Roads & Paths

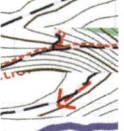

- Surfaced roads
- Dirt roads & tracks
- Walking trails
- Restricted/guided trails
- Obligatory walking direction
- Major hiking/trekking routes
- Downhill skiing routes & lifts

Natural Terrain

- Lakes, ponds
- Rivers; streams
- Waterfalls
- Wetland
- Wood
- Scrub
- Heath
- Meadow; grass
- Sand; beach
- Glacier
- Crevasse
- Cliffs; rocks; arete
- Scree; shingle
- Viewpoint
- Cave entrance

Man-made Features

- Farmland
- Orchard
- Power line
- Railroad

- Pipeline
- Quarry
- Wind turbine
- Radio mast, cell tower
- Lighthouse, buoy
- Cemetery
- Church

Amenities & Tourist Attractions

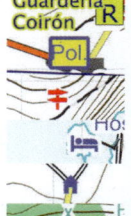

- Rangers post
- Police station; border control
- Tourist information
- Hotel, hostel
- Guest house; alpine hut; shelter
- Established campground; also staffed, commercial or otherwise regulated campsite
- Closed campsite
- Hospital
- Pharmacy
- Post office
- Playground
- Bank, ATM
- Monument, tourist attraction
- Museum

Transportation & Transport Amenities

- Car parking
- Fuel station
- Bus station/hub
- Bus stop
- Ferry & cruise ship routes
- Airport

Food & Water

- Cafe, restaurant, bakery
- Grocery store; supermarket
- Spring; drinking water fountain

All Elevations are in Meters

Mercator Projection

Sergio Mazitto Tourist Topo Maps

Available from
Amazon.com and other retailers

Γλαρονήσι

Δία
Dia

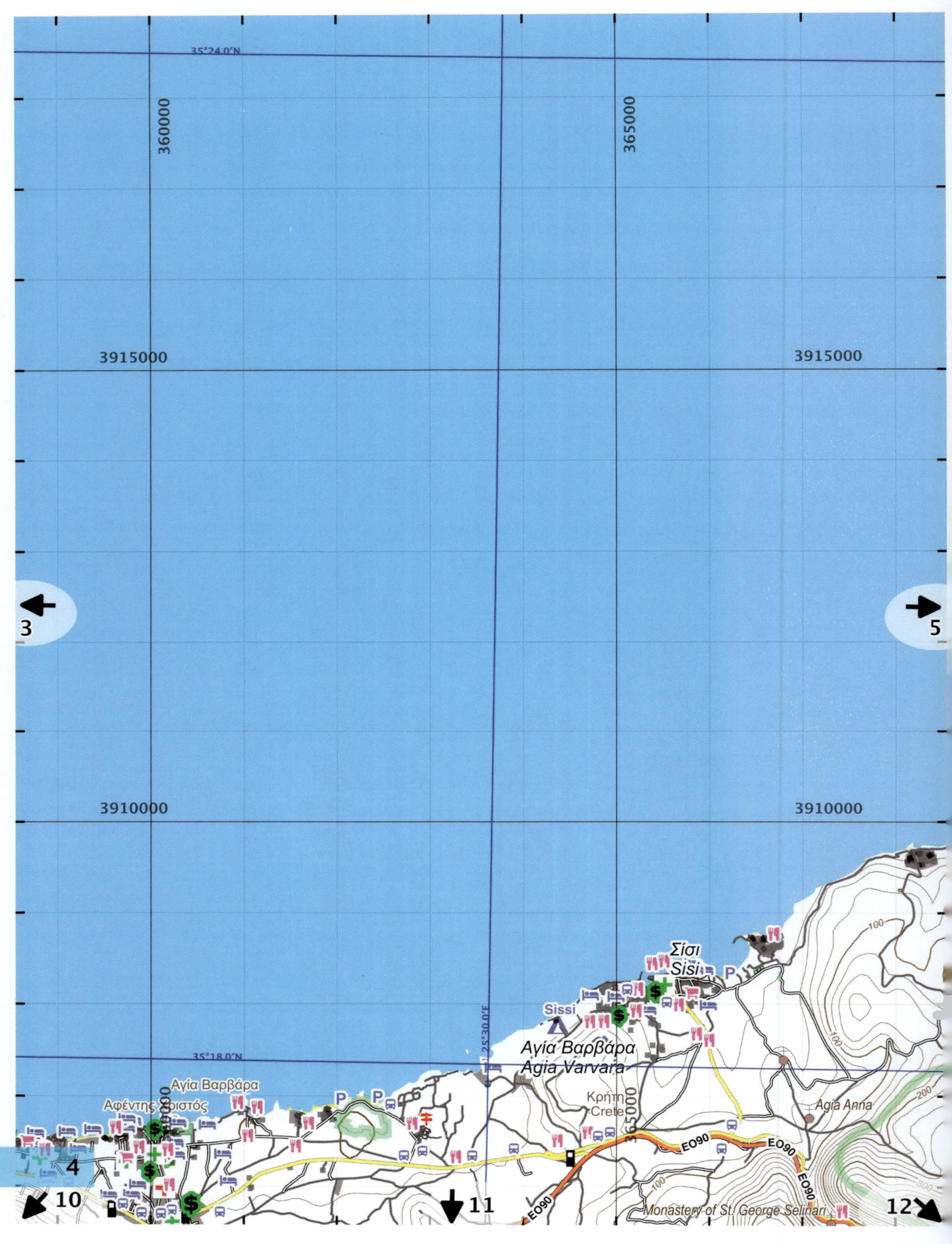

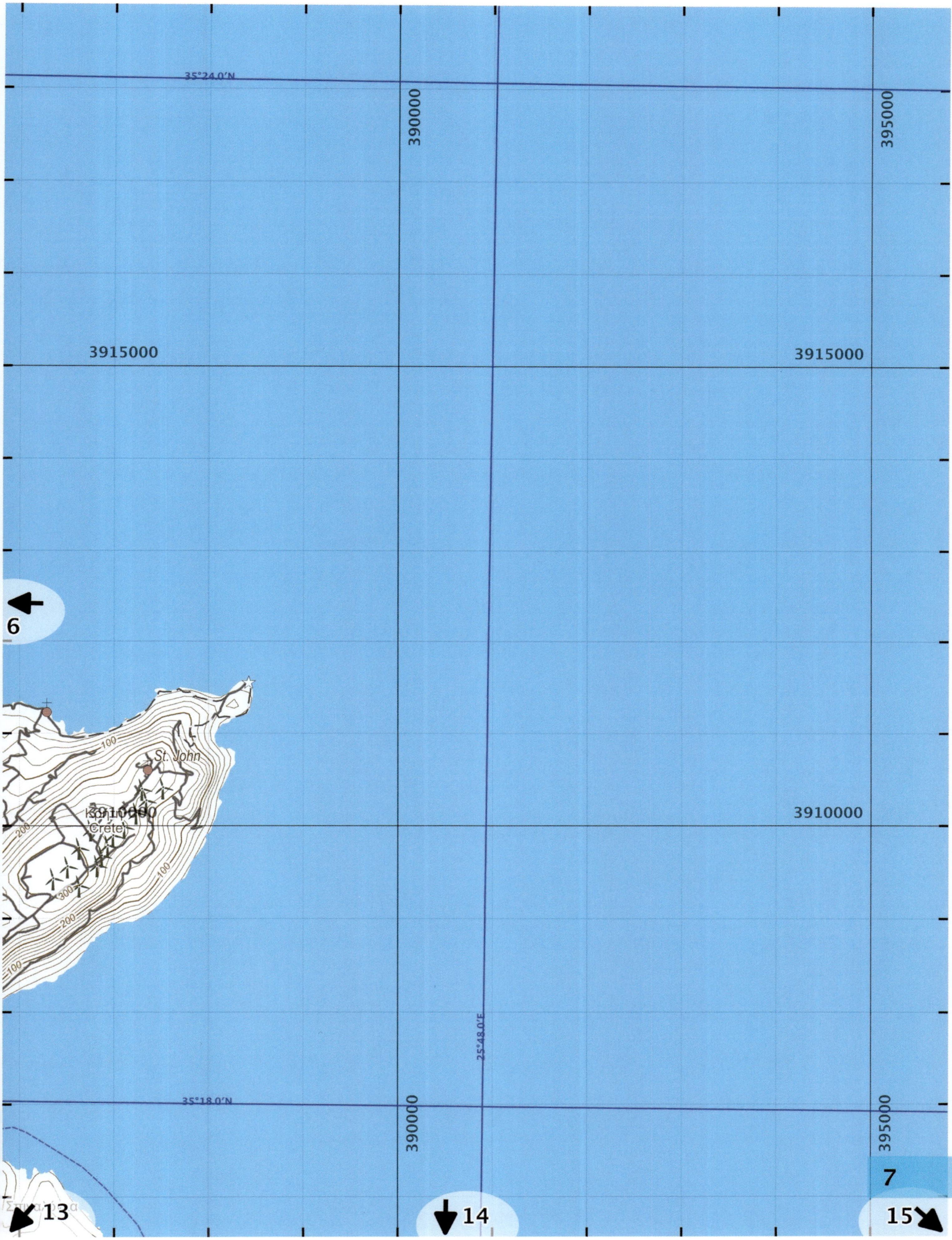

35°24.0'N

390000

395000

3915000   3915000

← 6

St. John

Koufonisi
(Crete)

3910000

25°48.0'E

35°18.0'N

390000   395000

↙13   ↓14   7   15↘

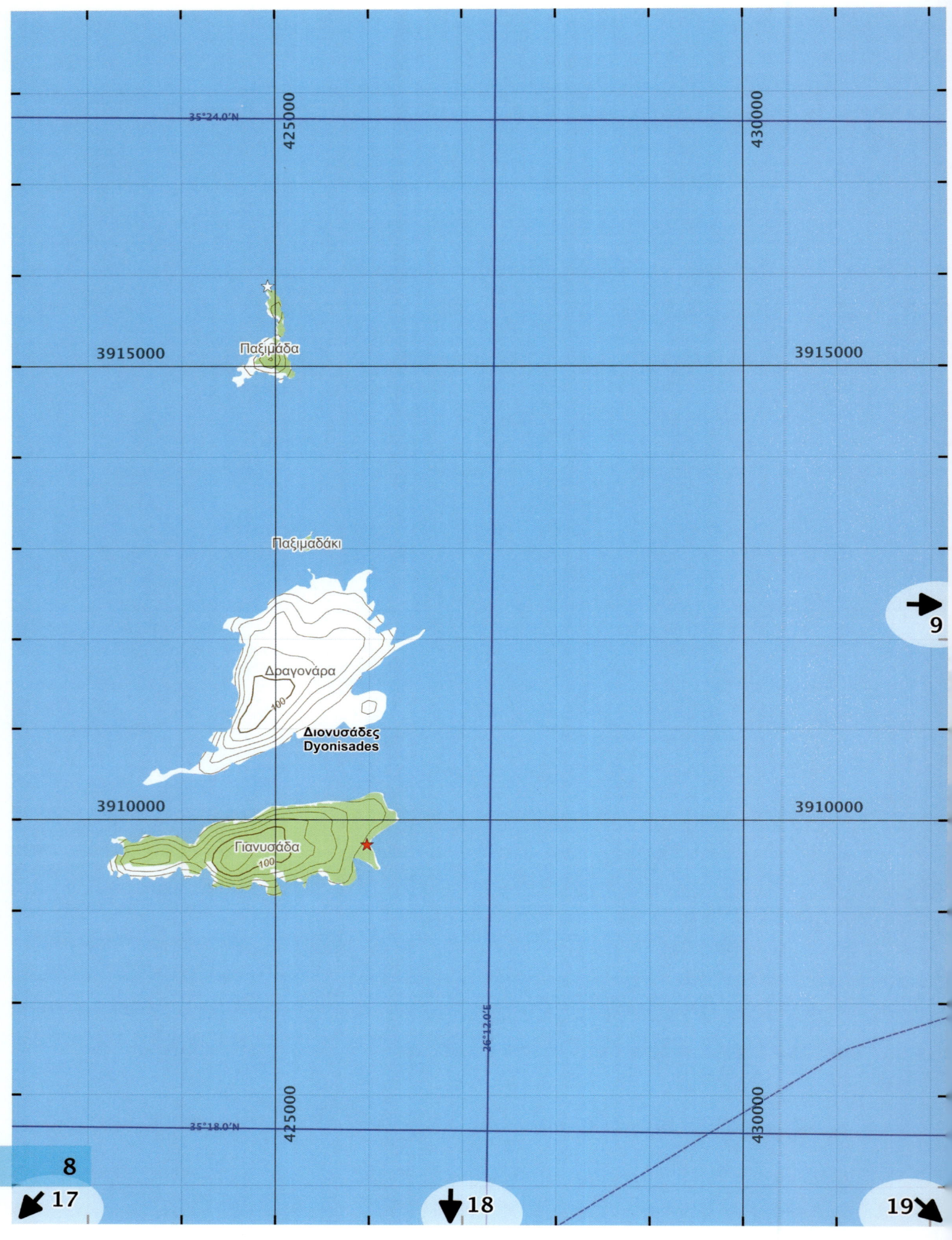

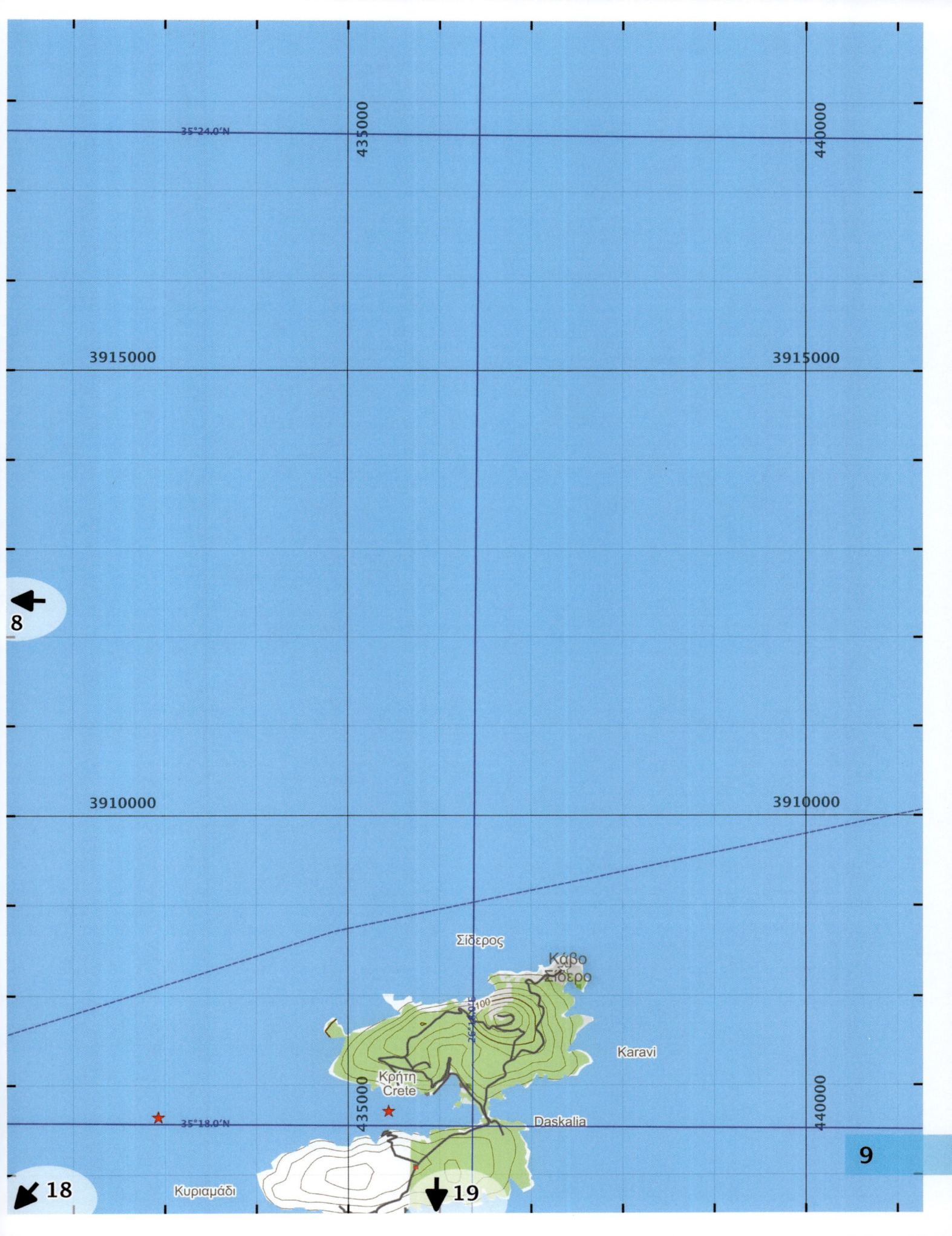

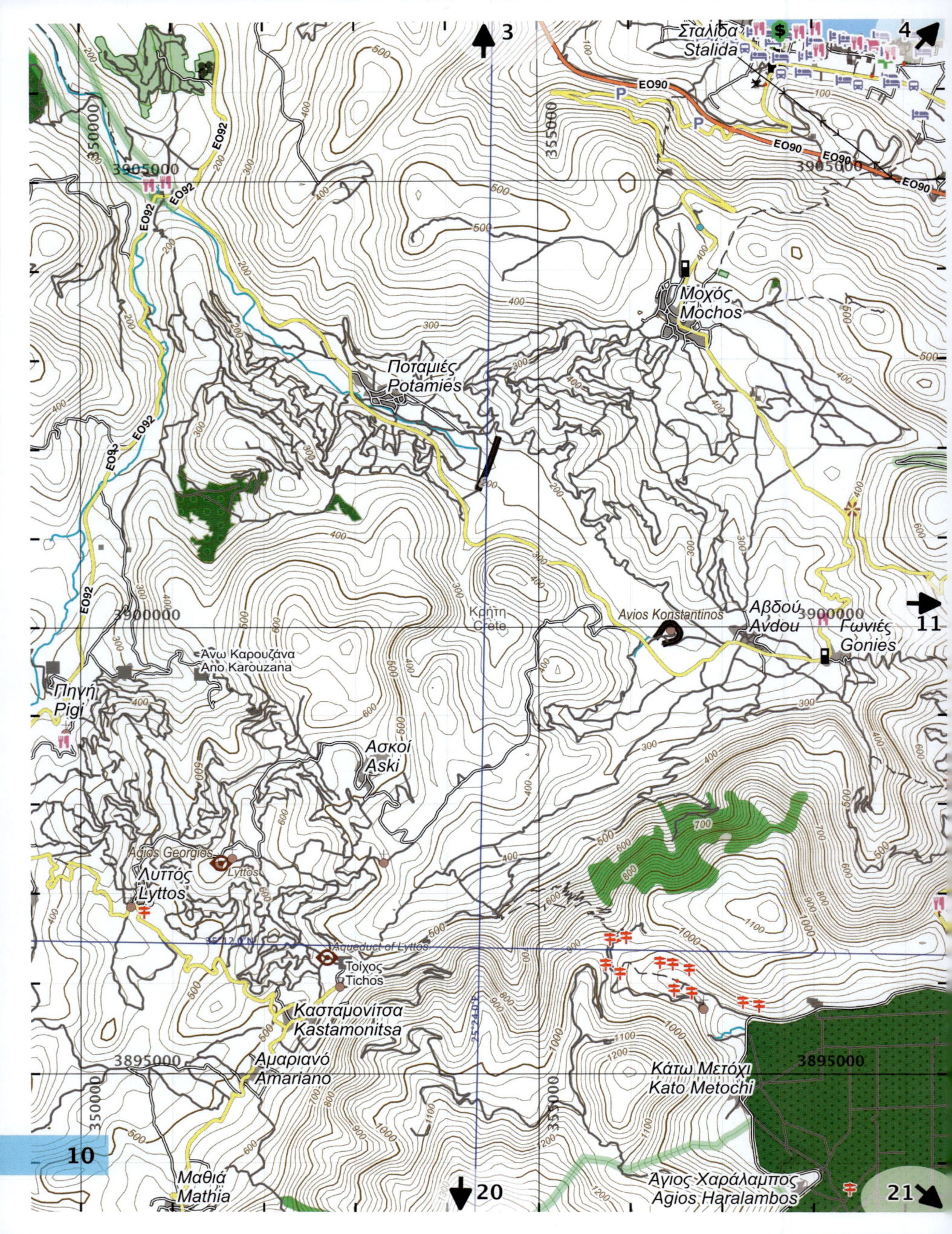

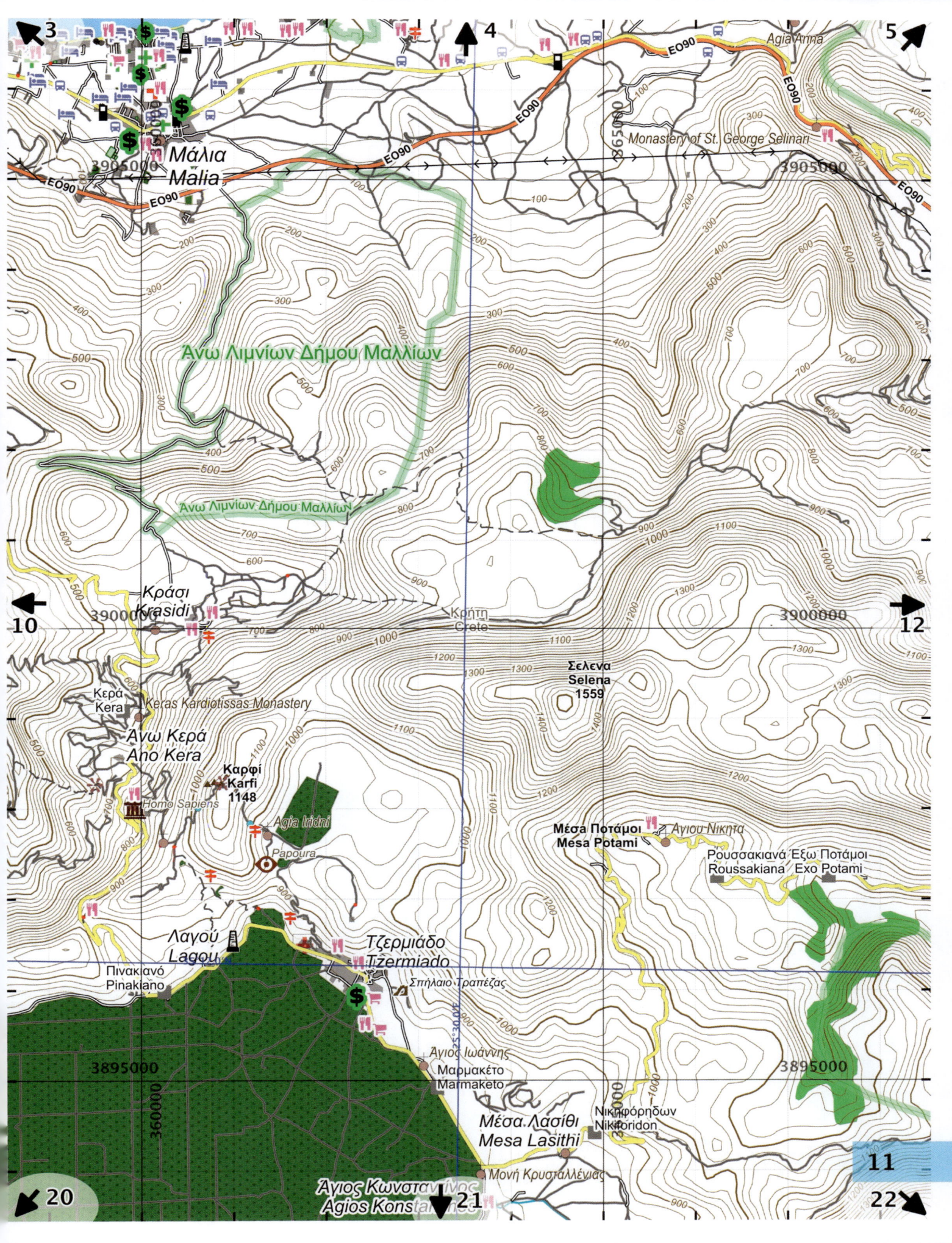

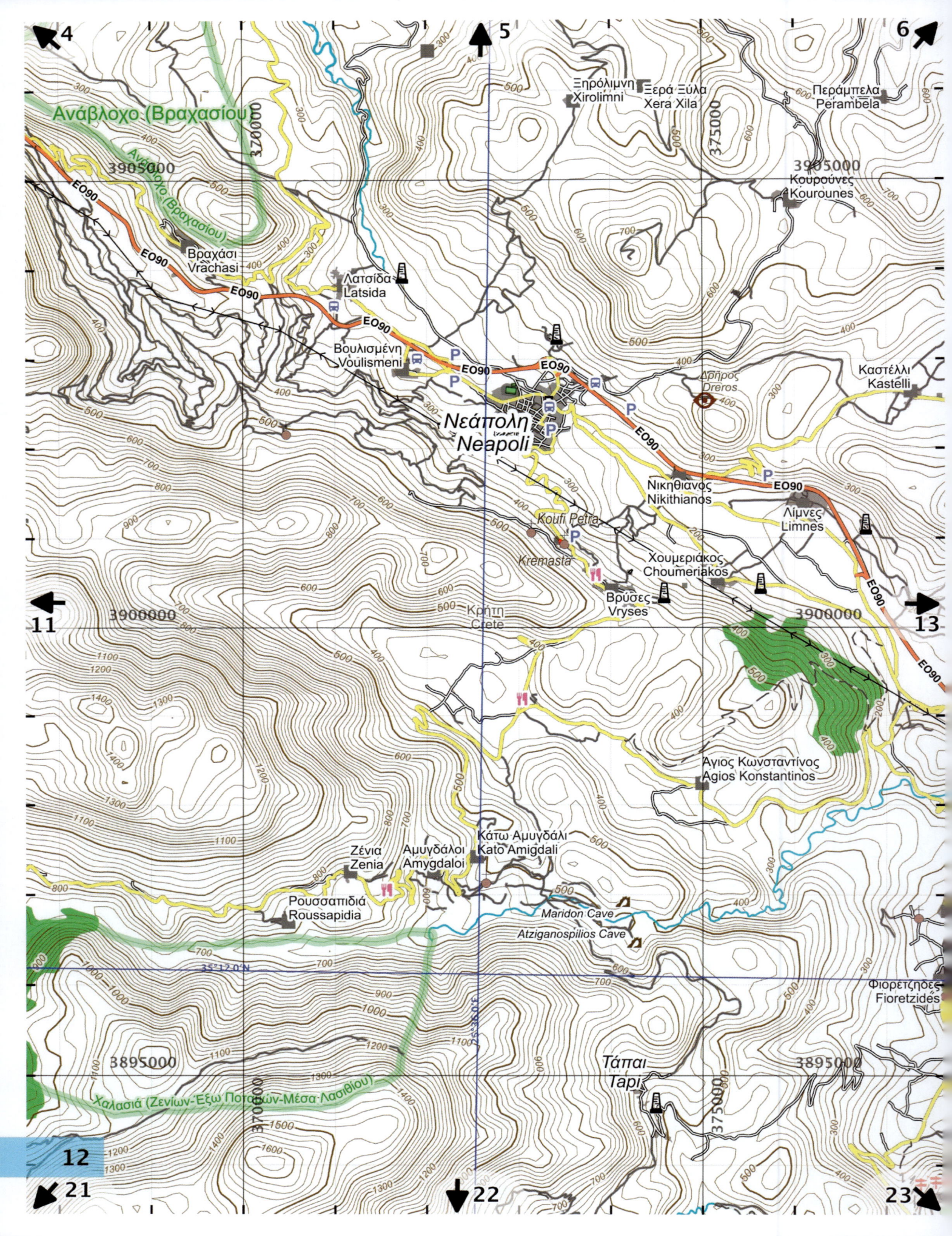

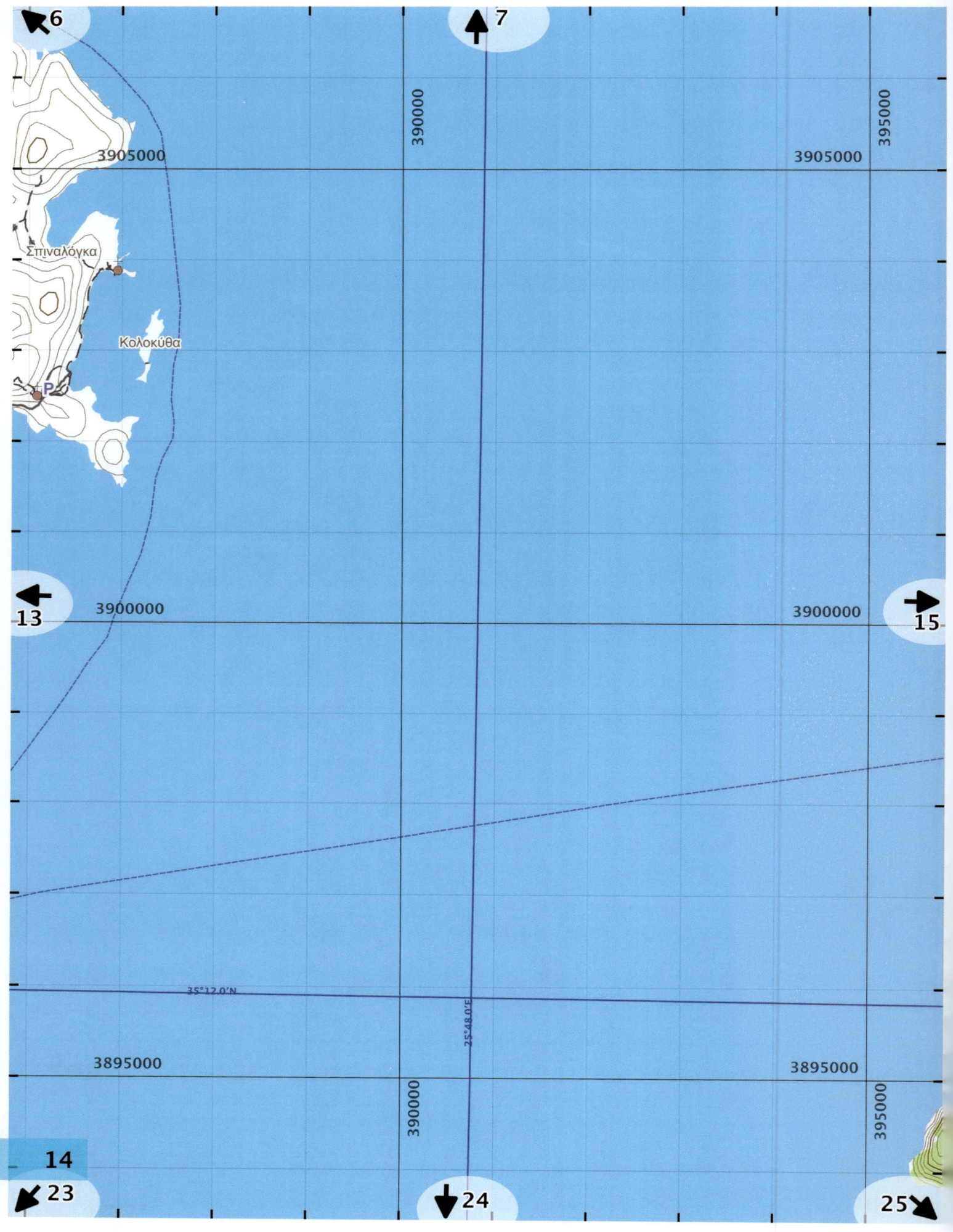

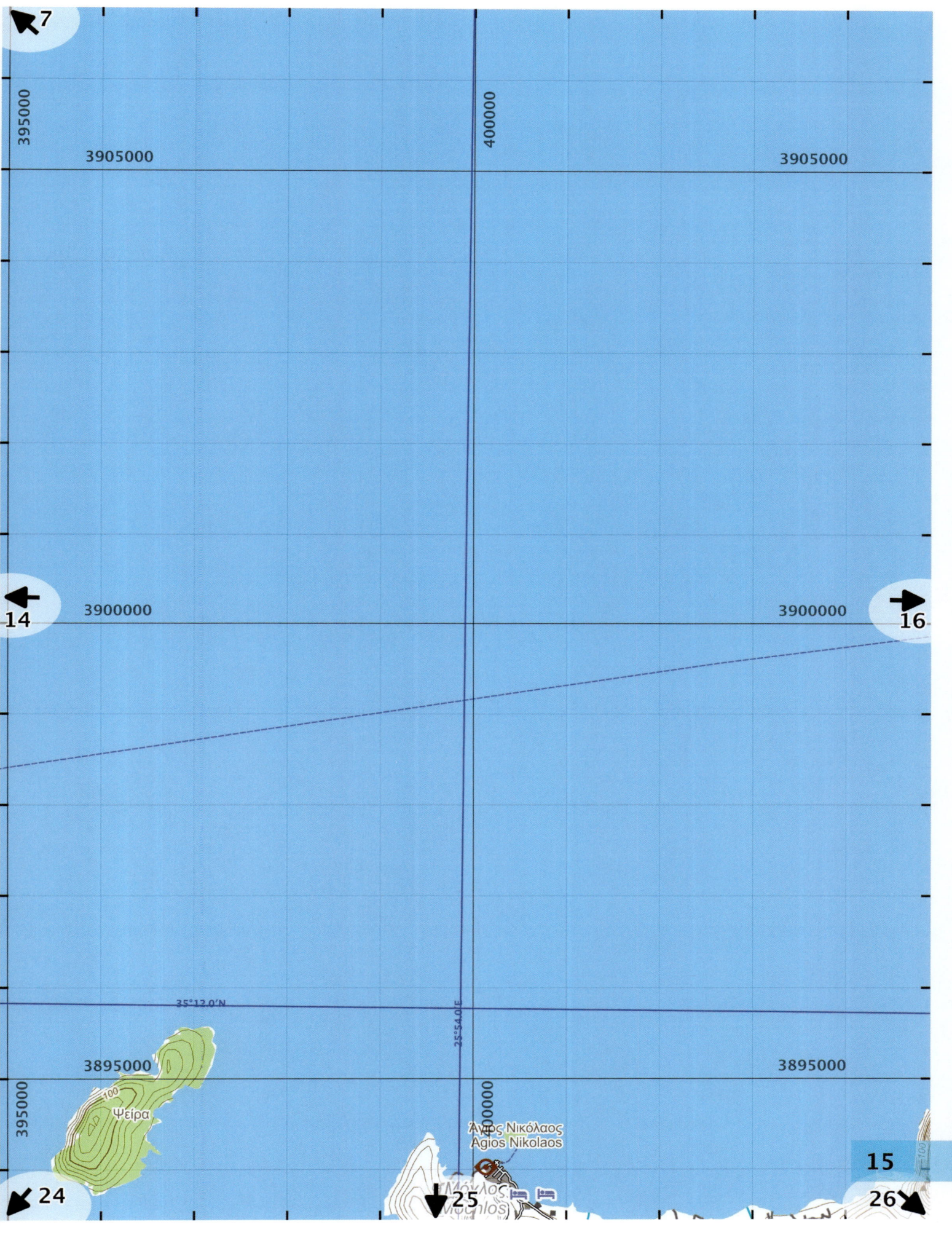

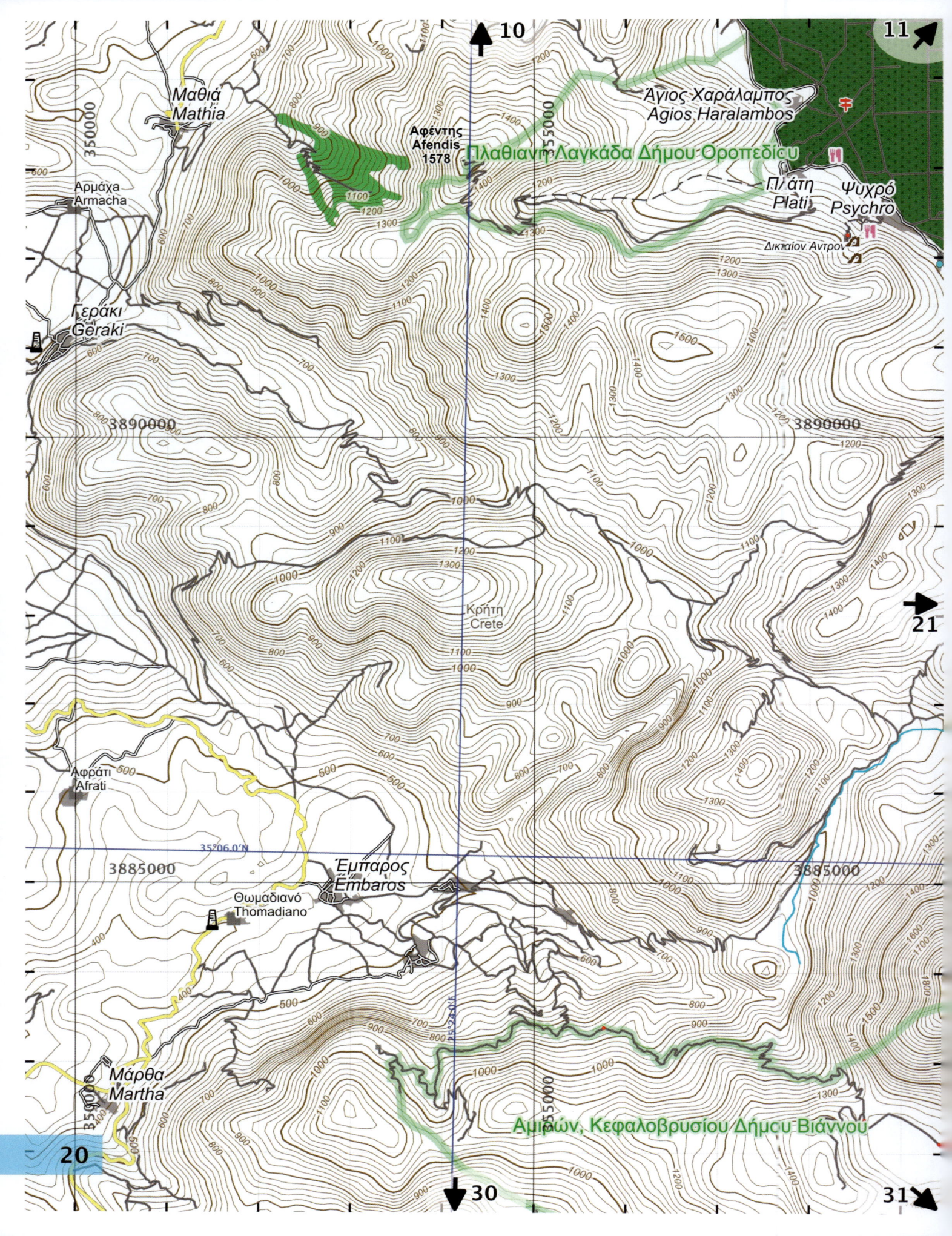

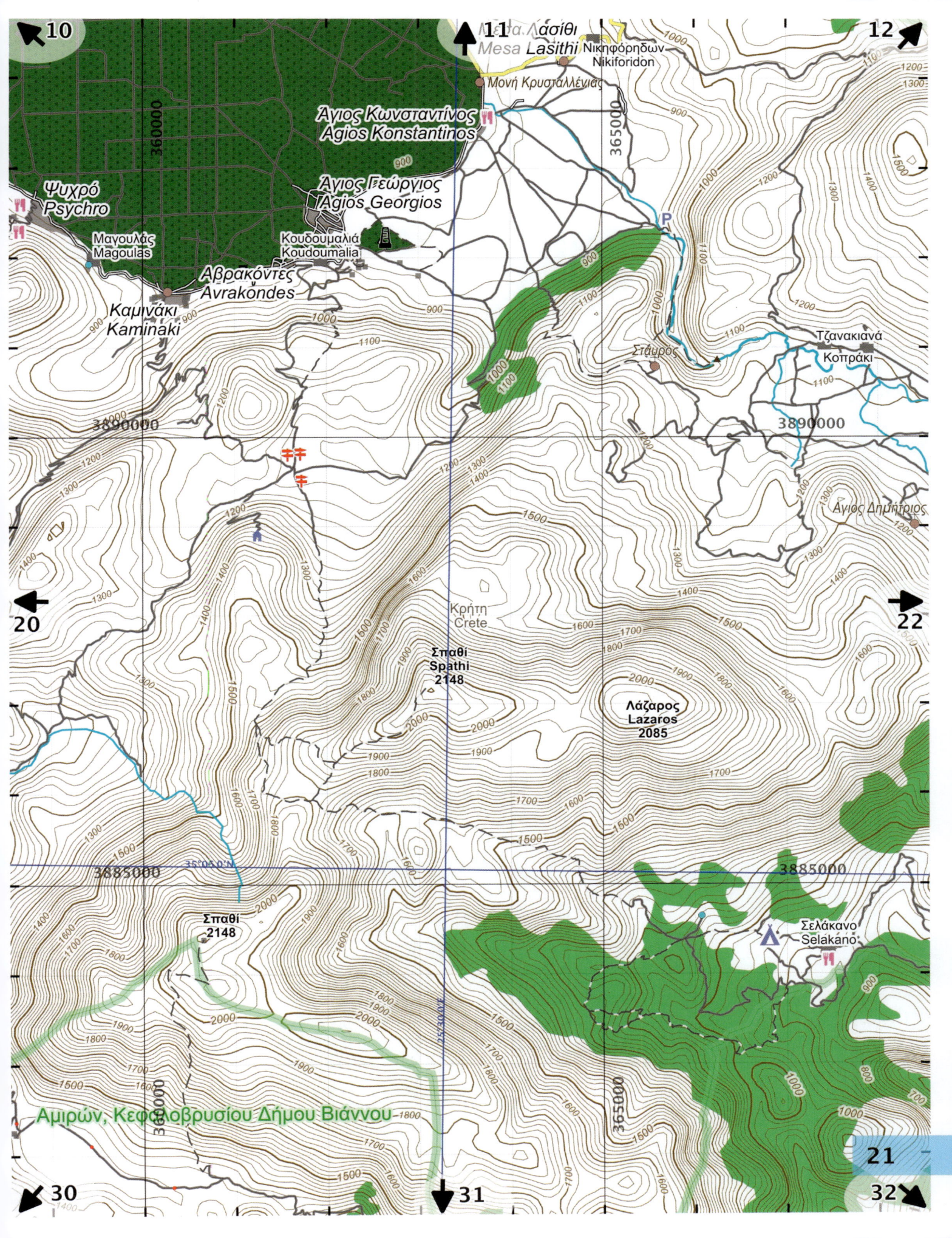

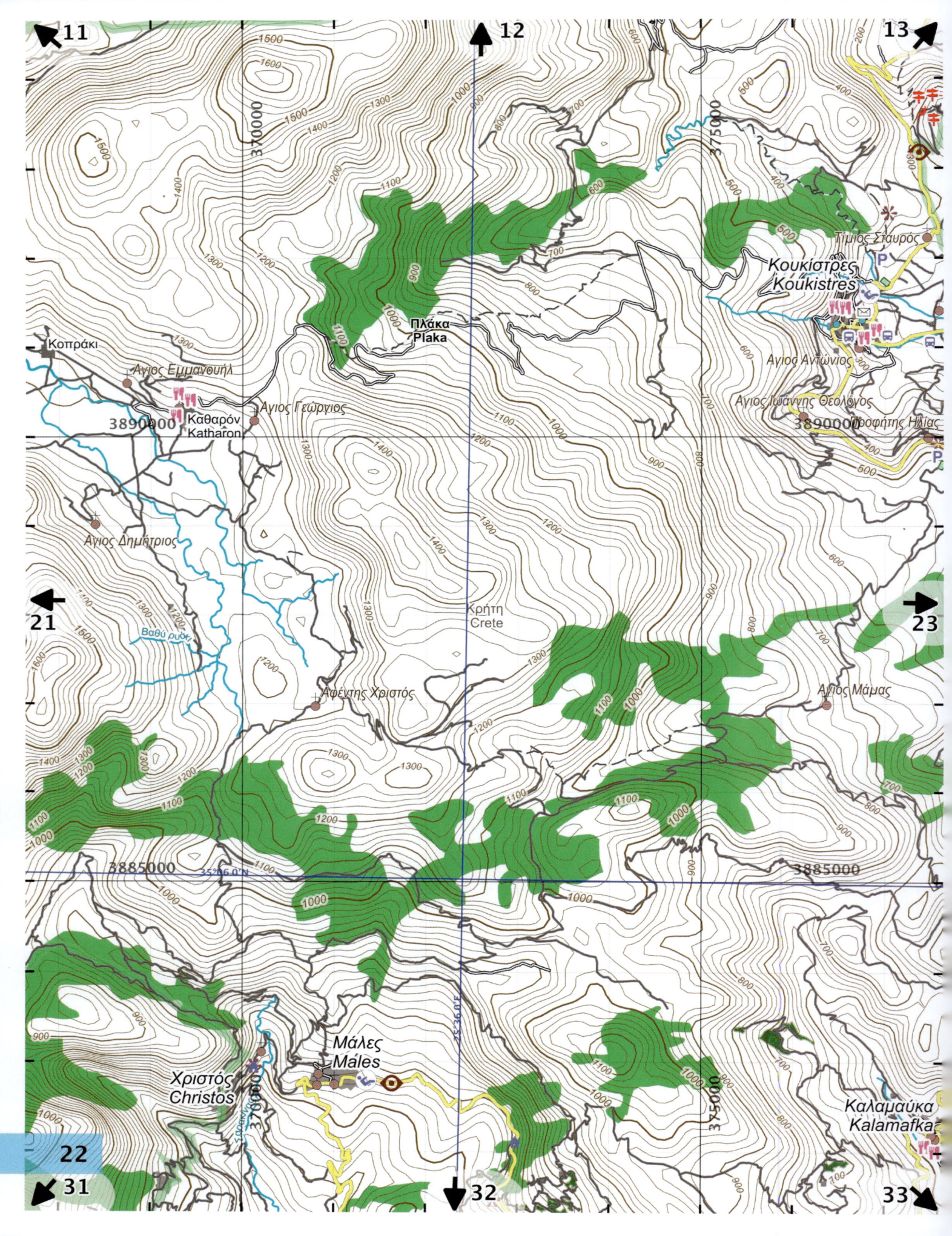

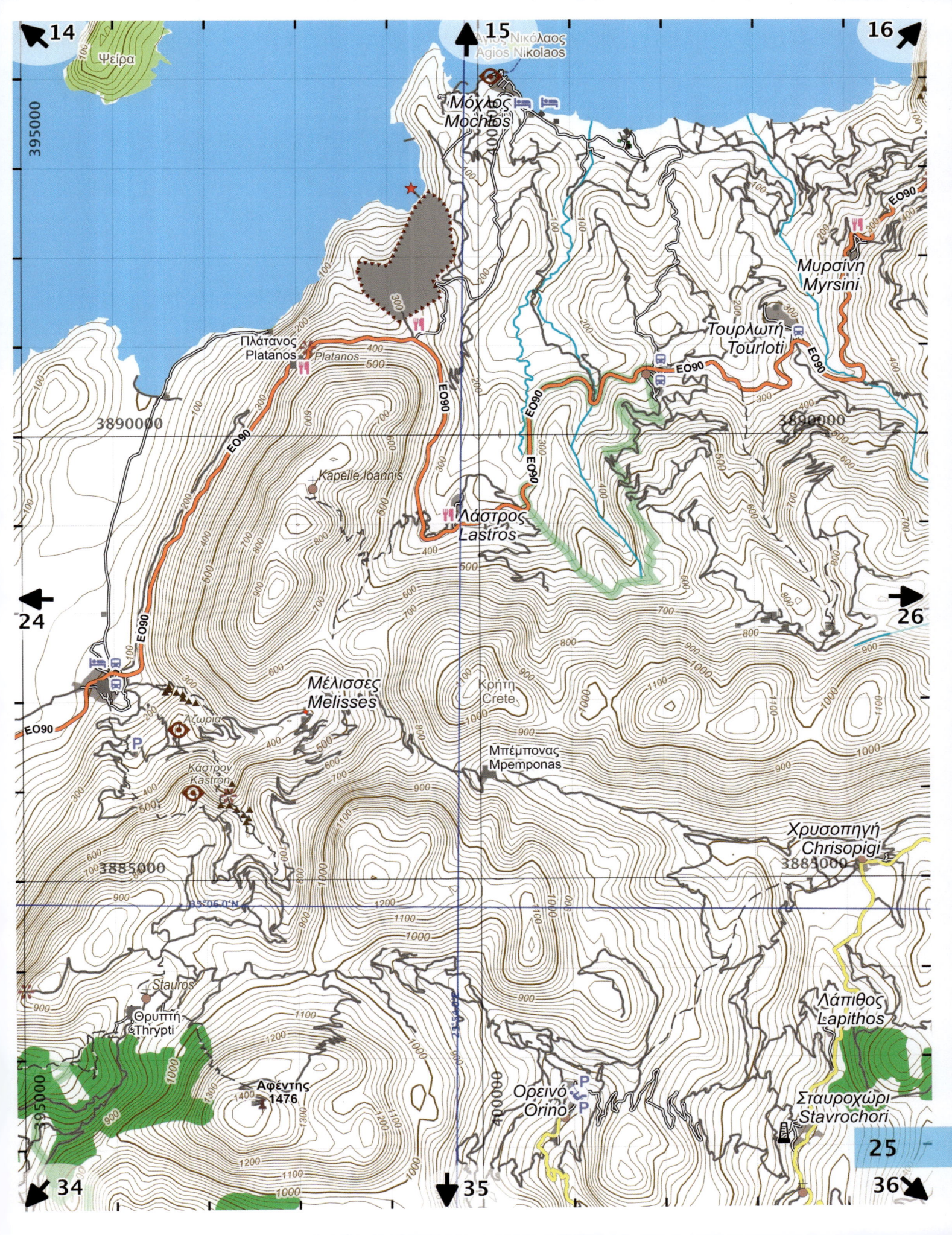

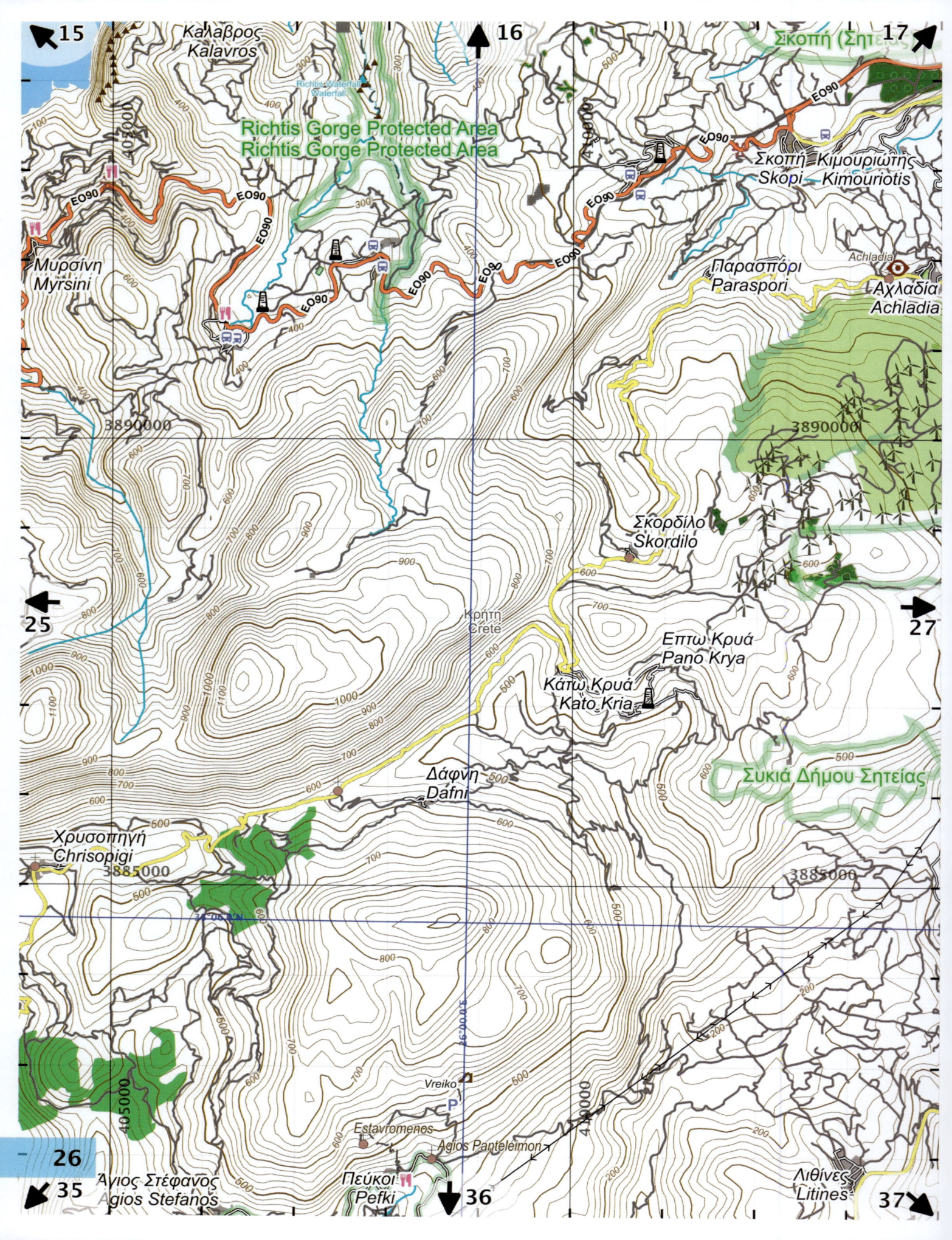

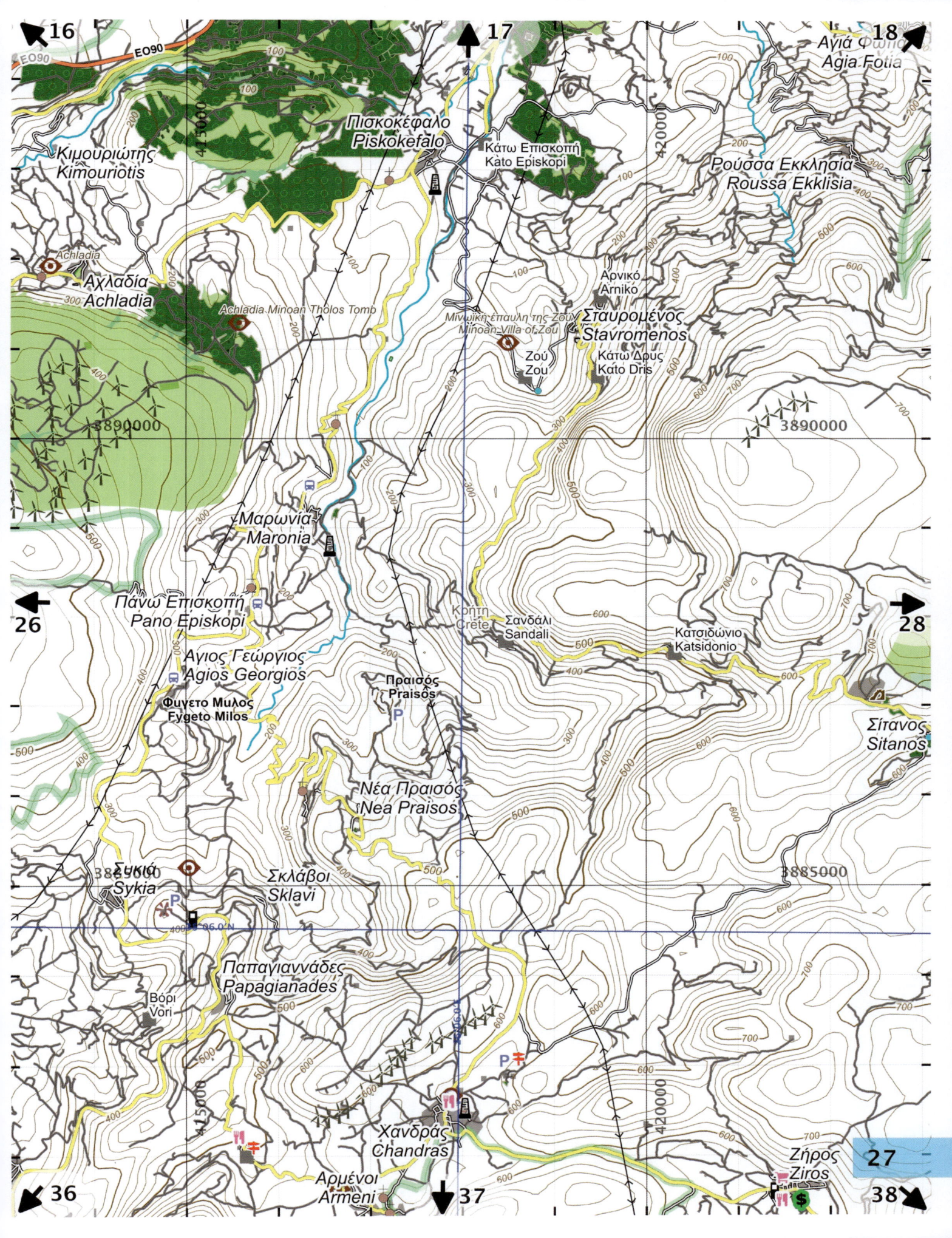

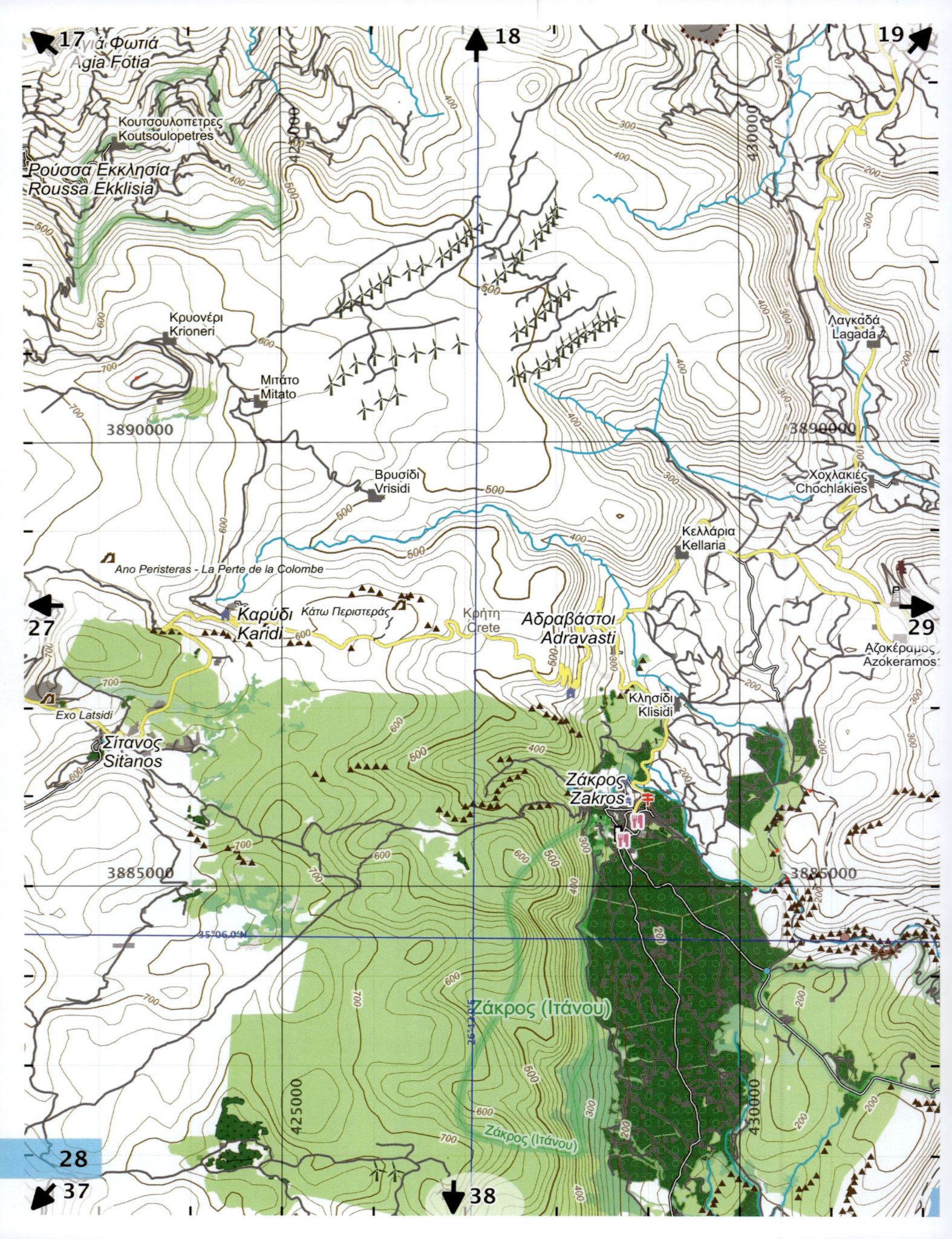

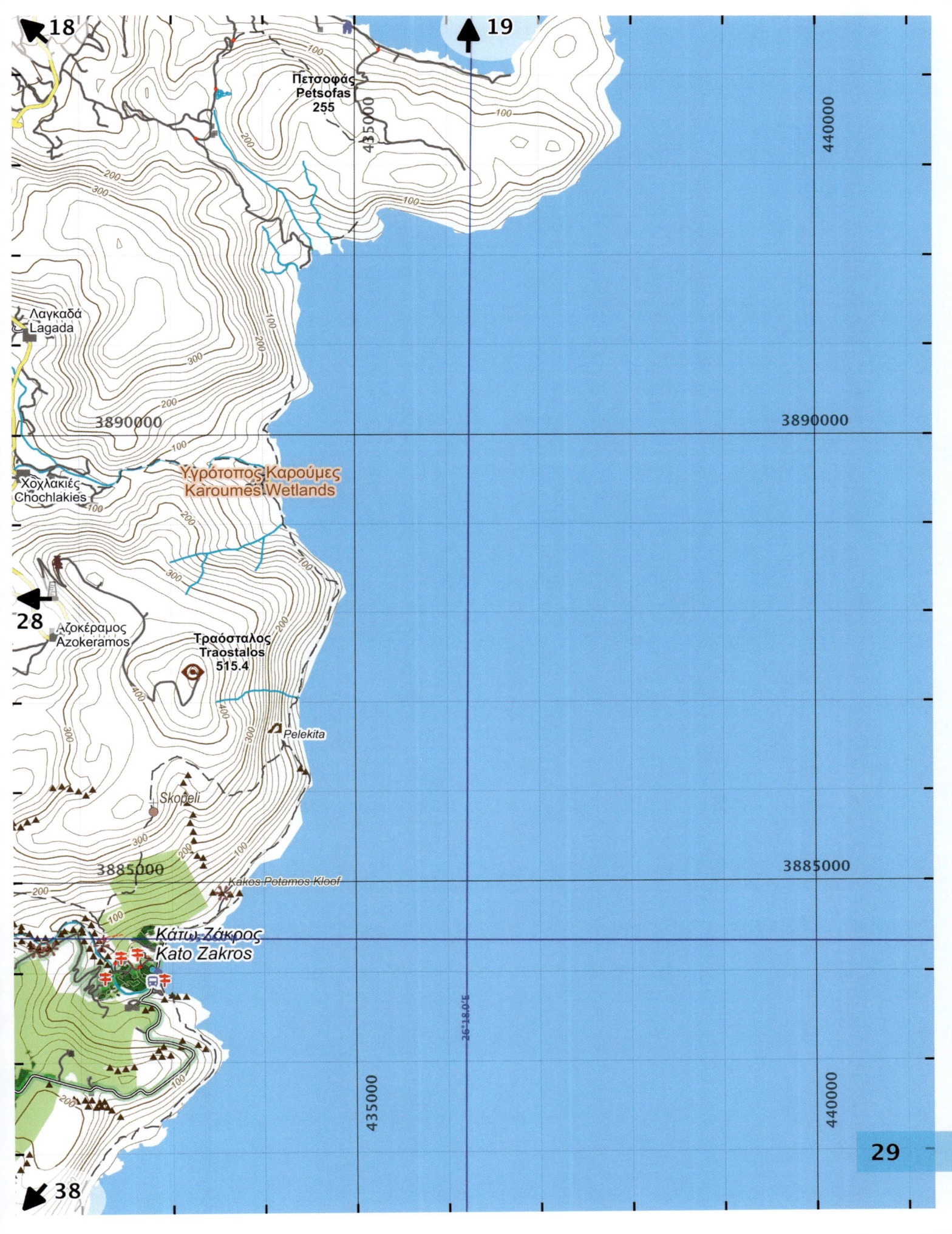

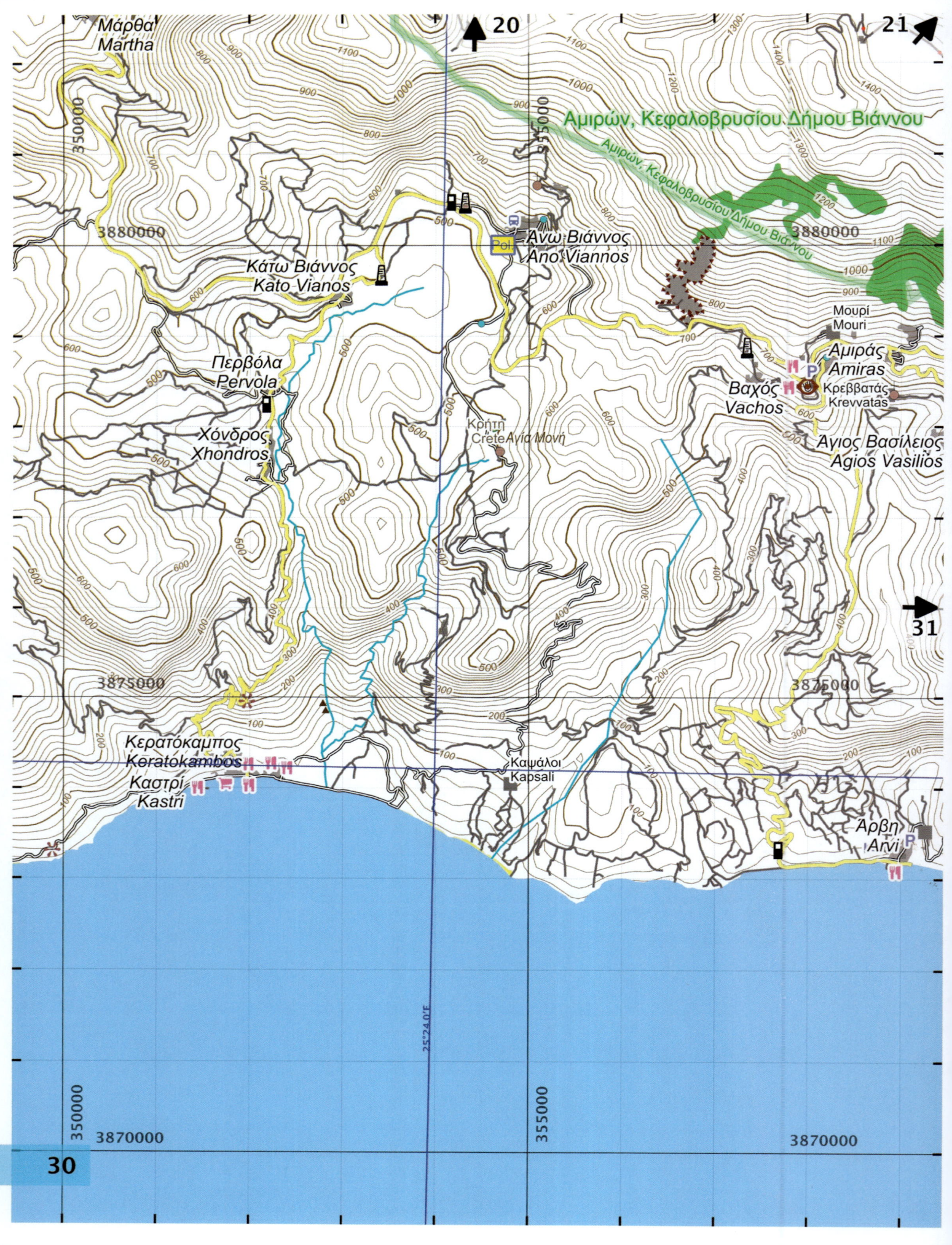

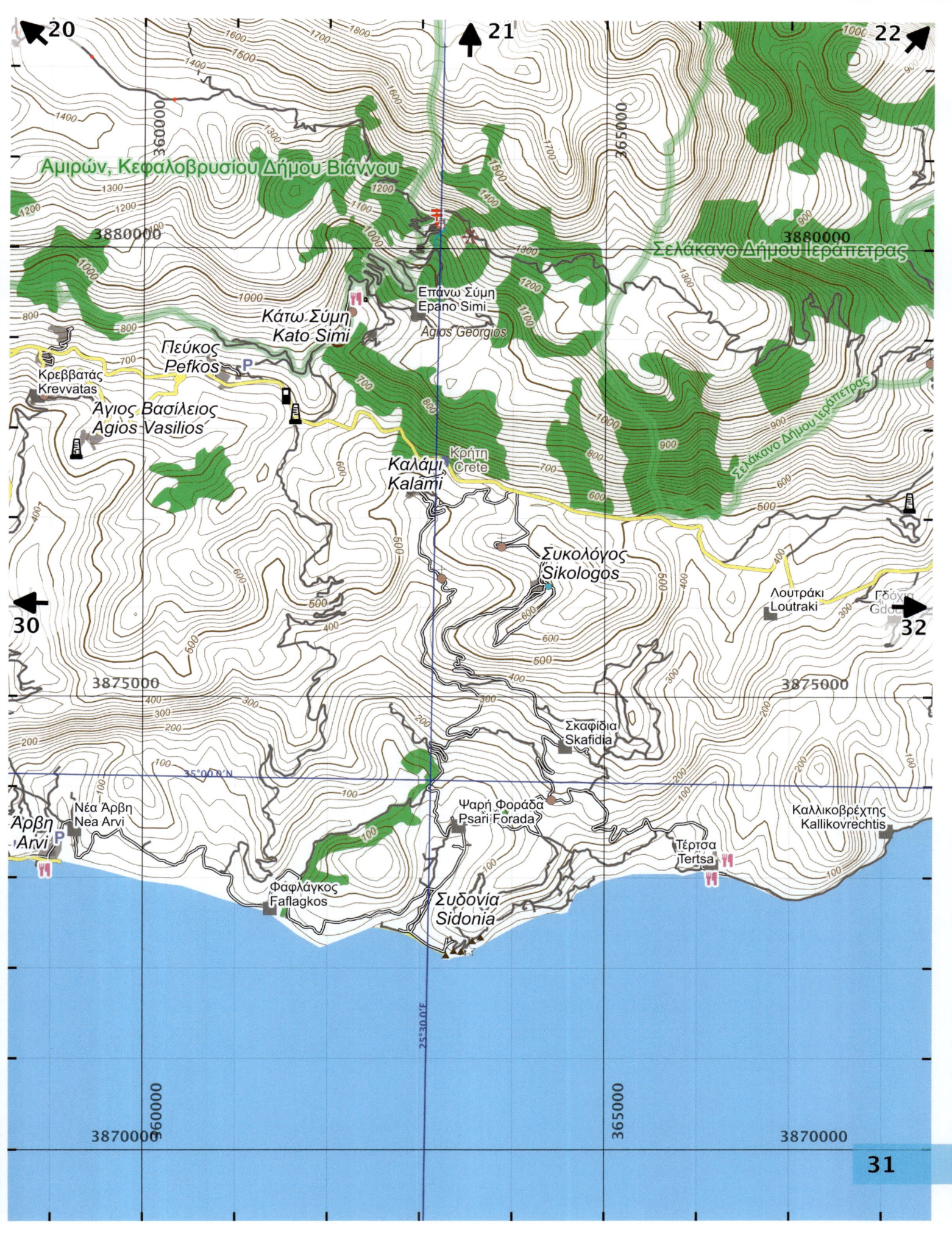

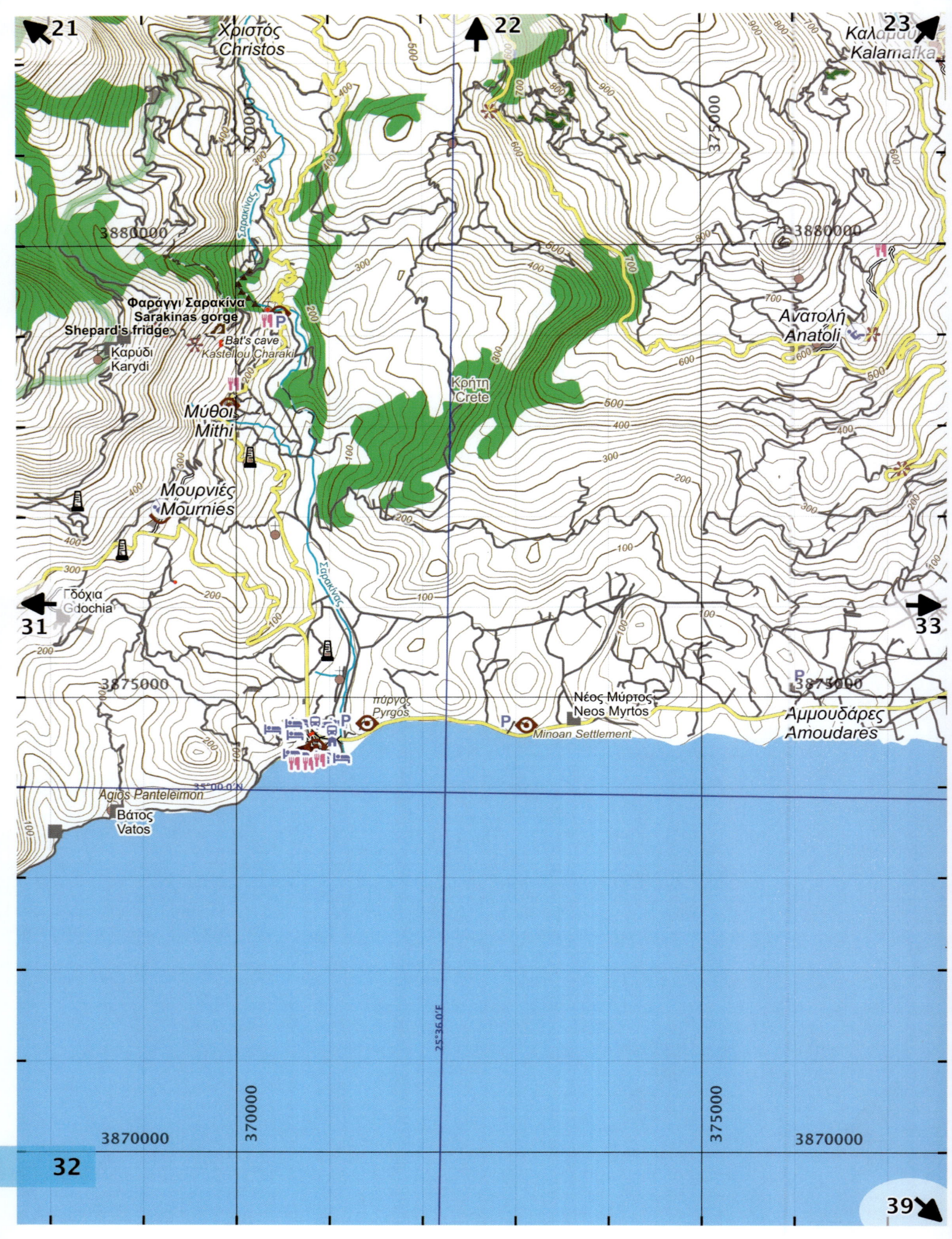

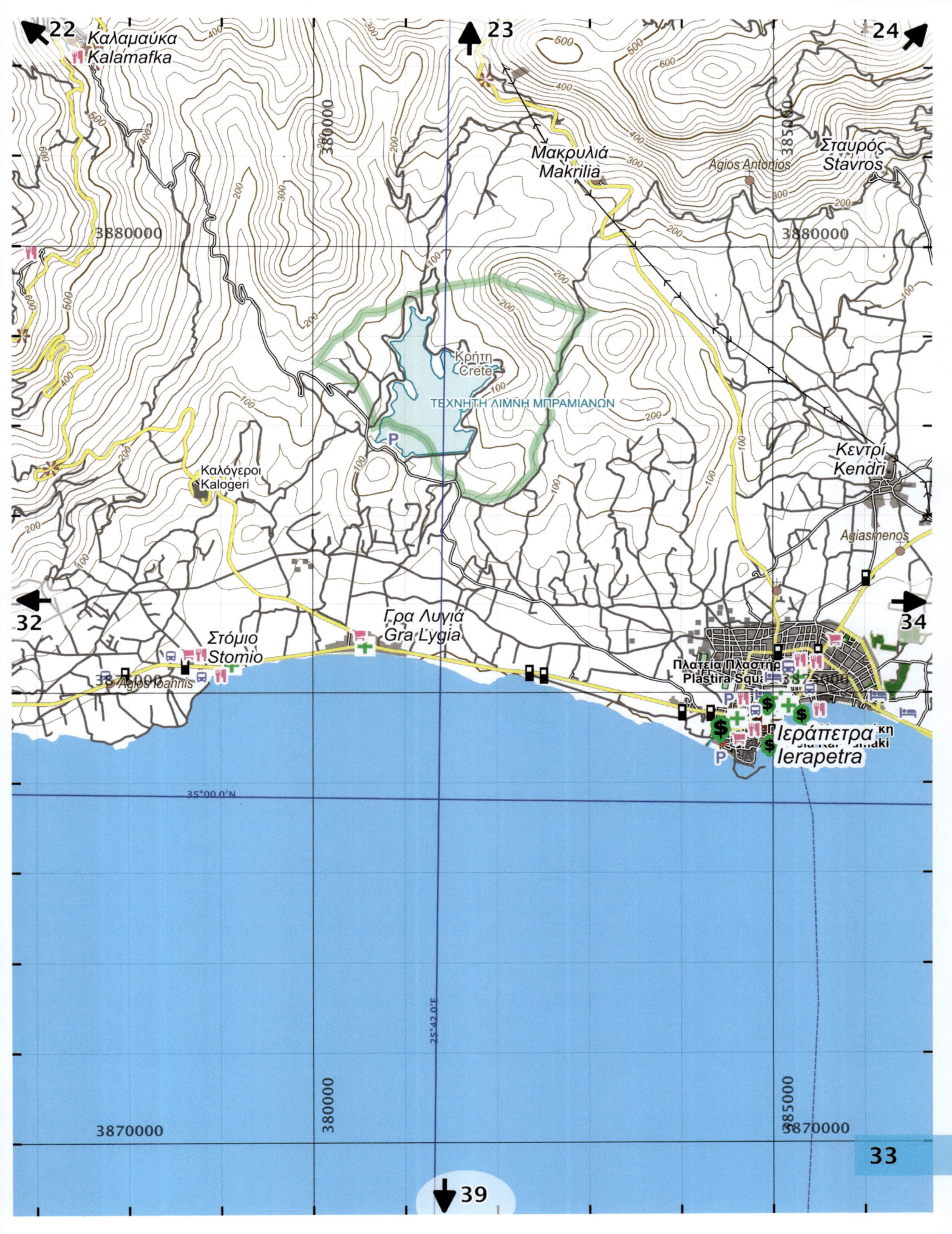

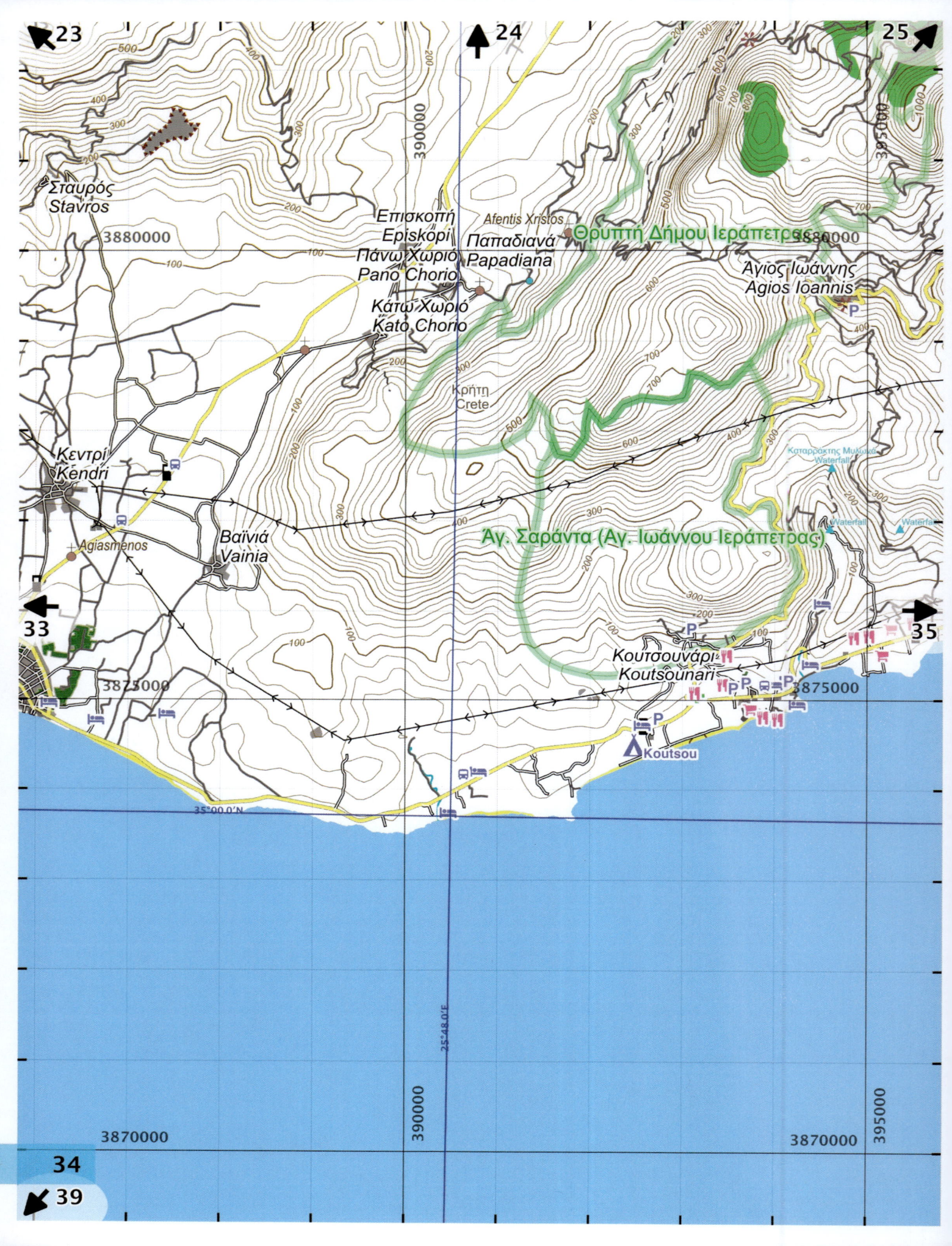

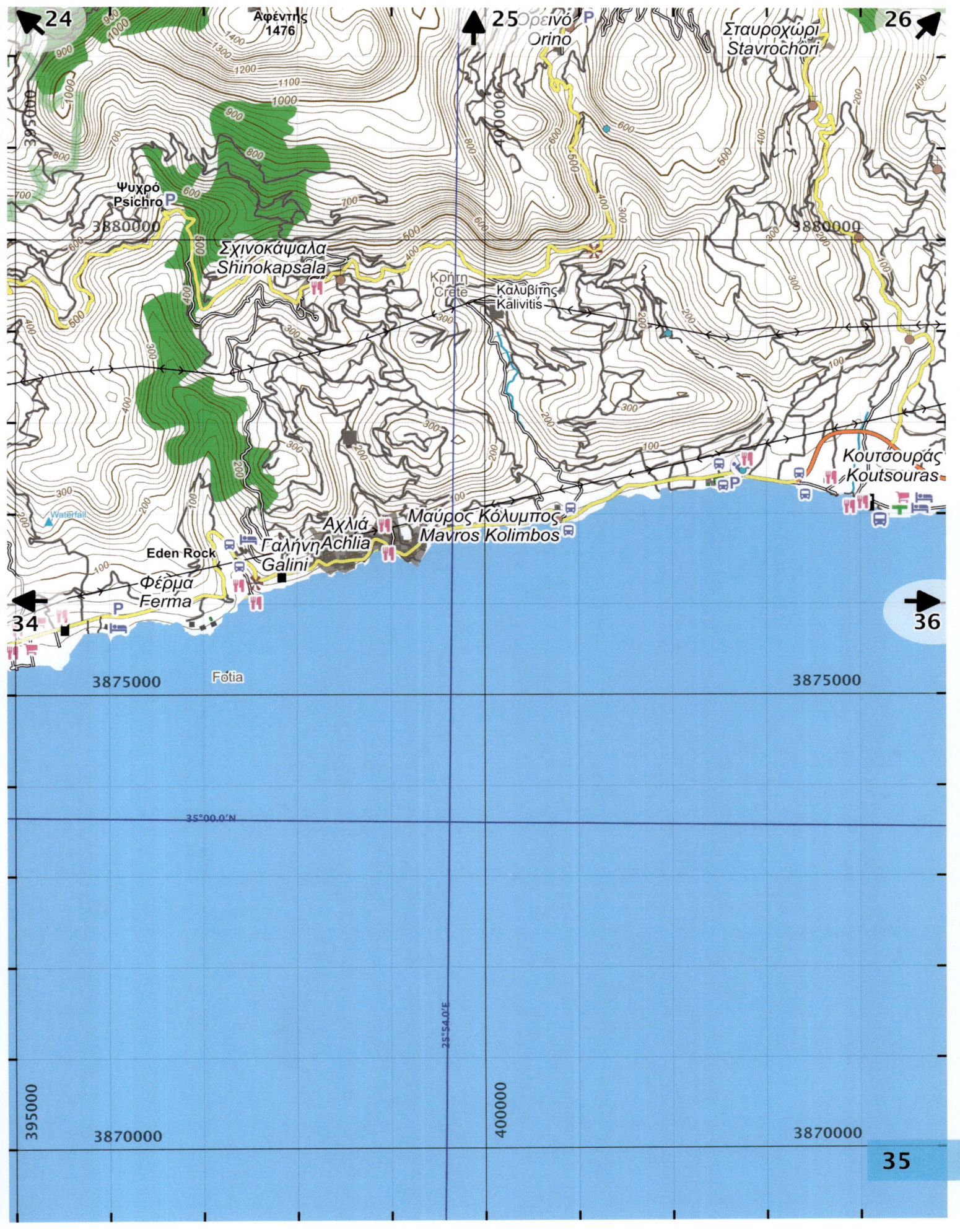

Νησί Χρυσή ή Γαϊδουρονήσι Chrissi

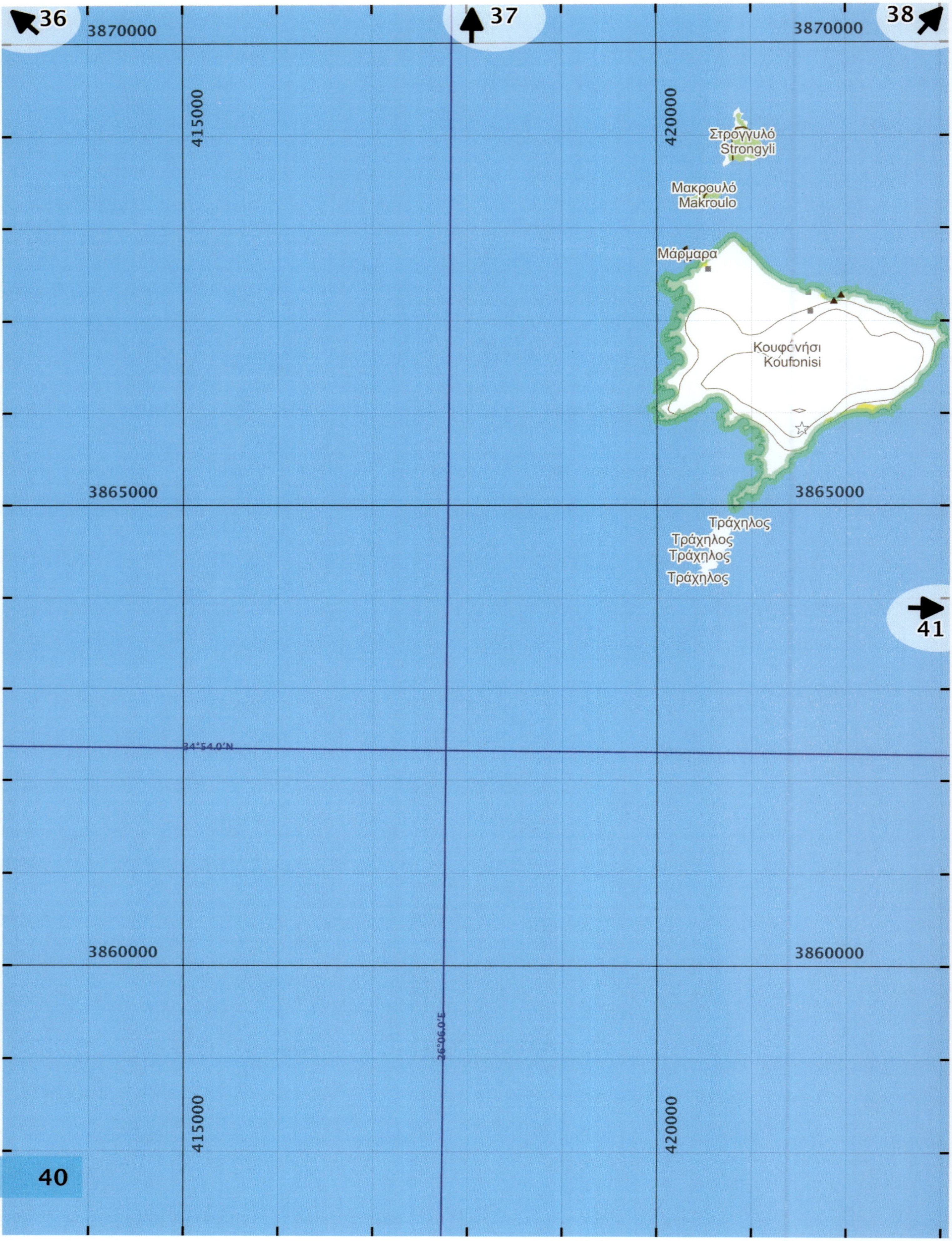

36
37
38
3870000
3870000
415000
420000
Στρογγυλό
Strongyli
Μακρουλό
Makroulo
Μάρμαρα
Κουφονήσι
Koufonisi
3865000
3865000
Τράχηλος
Τράχηλος
Τράχηλος
Τράχηλος
41
34°54.0'N
3860000
3860000
26°06.0'E
415000
420000

37

38

3870000

425000

430000

3870000

3865000

3865000

40

34°54.0'N

26°12.0'E

3860000

425000

430000

3860000

41

No Warranty: This map is provided to you "as is," and you agree to use it at your own risk. The publisher and its licensors make no guarantees, representations or warranties of any kind, express or implied, arising by law or otherwise, including but not limited to, content, quality, accuracy, completeness, effectiveness, reliability, merchantability, fitness for a particular purpose, usefulness, use or results to be obtained from this map product, This map product is intended to be used only as entertainment and a supplementary travel aid and must not be used for any purpose requiring precise measurement of direction, distance, location or topography. The publisher makes no warranty as to the accuracy or completeness of the map data in this map product.

Map & Atlas Design Copyright © Sergio Mazitto Topo Maps, 2018

Some map data Copyright © Openstreetmap contributors

Published by Sergio Mazitto

Printed in Great Britain
by Amazon